Look Inside a

Rubbish Bin

Louise Spilsbury

company incorporated in England and Wales having its registered office at 7 Pilgrim Street, London, EC4V 6LB – Registered company number: 6695582

www.raintre.co.uk
myorders@raintreepublishers.co.uk

Edited by Rebecca Rissman, Dan Nunn, and John-Paul Wilkins
Designed by Steve Mead
Original illustrations © Capstone Global Library Ltd 2013
Illustrations by Gary Hanna
Picture research by Ruth Blair
Production by Alison Parsons
Originated by Capstone Global Library Ltd
Printed and bound in China

ISBN 978 1 406 25127 2 (hardback)
16 15 14 13 12
10 9 8 7 6 5 4 3 2 1

ISBN 978 1 406 25134 0 (paperback)
17 16 15 14
10 9 8 7 6 5 4 3 2 1

British Library Cataloguing in Publication Data
Spilsbury, Louise.
Look inside a rubbish bin.
577.5'5-dc23
A full catalogue record for this book is available from the British Library.

We would like to thank the following for permission to reproduce photographs: iStockphoto p. 20 (© Alasdair Thomson); Naturepl pp. 11 (© Warwick Sloss), 12, 14, 15, 28 (© Stephen Dalton), 13 (© Rod Williams), 18 (© Adrian Davies), 19 (© Jason Smalley), 24, 26 (© Laurent Geslin), 27 (© Doug Wechsler); Science Photo Library p. 9 (DR JEREMY BURGESS); Shutterstock pp. 5 (© Zadiraka Evgenii), 6 (© Biehler, Michael), 7 (© sanddebeautheil), 8 (© plastique), 17 (© Martin Pot), 23 (© vicspacewalker), 25 (© Vladimir Chernyanskiy), 29 (© Pedro Miguel Sousa); Superstock p. 21 (© Pixtal).

Cover photograph of head of wasp in extreme close up with grey background, reproduced with permission of Shutterstock (© Biehler, Michael).

We would like to thank Michael Bright and Diana Bentley for their invaluable help in the preparation of this book.

Every effort has been made to contact copyright holders of any material reproduced in this book. Any omissions will be rectified in subsequent printings if notice is given to the publisher.

Disclaimer

Contents

Some words are shown in bold, **like this**. You can find out what they mean by looking in the glossary.

Down from above

Rubbish bins are **habitats** for some animals! They find food and **shelter** in and around bins. Some animals fly down from above to feed.

Pigeons high up on buildings keep a look out for food to eat. If they see an open rubbish bin, they can fly down to feed on waste, such as breadcrumbs.

▲ Lots of pigeons live in cities.

Wasps like to eat sweet liquids. These stripy **insects** use their **antennae** to find food. In late summer, they buzz around rubbish bins in search of leftover fizzy drinks or sticky juices from rotting fruit.

▼ Wasps smell with their two antennae.

antennae

▲ A wasp licks up its lunch!

Wasps lap up food using their short tongues. Make sure you don't bother a wasp while it is feeding! It can give a painful sting using a sharp stinger at the end of its body.

Flies also smell food rotting in rubbish bins. They sit on the waste and spit on it to make it go soft. Then they suck it up with a long tube called a **proboscis**.

▼ Flies suck up their food!

proboscis

▲ A female fly laying her eggs.

Female flies lay tiny white eggs on rotting food, too. Then their young will have something tasty to eat when they **hatch** out.

At the top

Some animals visit the top of a rubbish bin to find food or **shelter**. Other animals are born at the top of the bin.

Tiny **maggots hatch** from flies' eggs on rotting food. They eat and grow bigger until they turn into adult flies. Then they fly away, maybe to another rubbish bin!

▲ Wriggling maggots search for food.

Rats climb inside rubbish bins. They have sharp claws to get a grip and a long tail for balance. Rats can see well in the dark and have a good sense of smell to sniff out food to eat.

▼ Rubbish bins are full of treats for a rat.

Rats eat almost anything. They have large front teeth that they use to **gnaw** into containers to get at the food inside. They can even gnaw through tins!

This rat is nibbling an apple. ▶

Cockroaches visit rubbish bins to find food, too. These **insects** have tough, flat bodies that can squeeze through small gaps. Spikes on their legs help them get a grip as they crawl along.

▼ Cockroaches love food waste!

▲ This cockroach is on the scent of some rubbish.

Cockroaches use their long **antennae** to smell food. They also follow trails left by other cockroaches. Cockroaches leave a trail of smelly poo as they crawl through waste.

Deep inside

Deep inside a rubbish bin it is dark. It is also damp because liquid from the rotting waste trickles down from above. Some of the animals here help to break down the waste.

Woodlice like damp, dark places. They have 14 legs that they use to crawl around over rubbish. They chomp away at waste cardboard and wood.

▲ Woodlice can sniff out food from a bin.

A slug has no legs. It makes a slippery trail of **mucus** to slide along through the rubbish. It stretches and pulls its soft body over the mucus to move around.

▼ Slugs slide along on their own slime.

▲ Slugs scrape off bits of food waste to eat.

Slugs have a tongue rather like a
cheese grater! They rub it on waste food
such as old cabbage leaves to break
off pieces they can eat.

Worms live in the dark, damp sludge at the bottom of some rubbish bins. They wriggle inside through cracks using bristles on the bottom of their bodies. Worms like damp places because they can die if their skin dries out.

▼ Red worms are often called red wrigglers!

▲ Worms help to get rid of waste.

Worms burrow through waste and eat old food like eggshells and used tea bags. They do not have teeth so they wait until food softens and eat little bits at a time. Big groups of worms help to break down waste.

Around the bin

Food waste that spills out of full rubbish bins is a tempting treat for some animals. Other animals wait near bins to hunt the animals that feed or live there.

Stray cats have no owners to feed them. They have to find their own food to survive. They often hunt for **prey** that lives on waste, such as rats and pigeons.

▲ Stray cats often find prey near bins.

Foxes mostly visit rubbish bins at **dusk** when people are indoors. They are **scavengers** and especially like to eat waste meat, such as chicken bones and half-eaten burgers.

▼ Rubbish is like fast food for a fox!

▲ This cub is returning to its den.

Some foxes make their homes near rubbish bins so they do not have to go far to find food. They dig **dens** in the mud under garden sheds or bushes. They also raise their cubs there.

Gulls may catch fish to eat at the seaside, but in cities they are mostly **scavengers**. They eat all sorts of rubbish, from dirty rags to crusts of bread. They may even eat a cockroach or two!

▼ These gulls are looking for waste to eat.

▲ Gulls collect food for their chicks.

Gulls make nests on the roofs of buildings in towns and cities. Hungry chicks peck their parent's beak to make them cough up some of the food they have eaten.

Rubbish bin habitats

People throw away lots of food. Different animals around the world visit rubbish bins because it is easy to find something to eat there. What animals can you spot around the bins near where you live?

▼ Raccoons in America often raid rubbish bins.

▲ Hungry gulls visit rubbish tips looking for food.

Waste in rubbish bins soon goes smelly and bad. Lorries take waste to giant rubbish tips. Many animals live or visit these tips to eat food waste. When you throw away food, you might be providing a meal for animals in a rubbish bin **habitat**!

Glossary

antennae (singular: antenna) thin parts on the head of some animals, including beetles and lobsters, that are used to feel and touch

den hidden home or resting place of some animals, such as badgers or bears

dusk time of day just before night

female sex of an animal or plant that is able to produce eggs or seeds. Females are the opposite sex to males.

gnaw bite or chew again and again

habitat place where particular types of living things are likely to live. For example, polar bears live in snowy habitats and camels live in desert habitats.

hatch come out of an egg

insect type of small animal that has three body parts, six legs, and usually wings. Ants and dragonflies are types of insect.

maggot young stage in the life cycle of a fly

mucus slime

prey animal that is caught and eaten by another animal

proboscis special mouth part of some insects used to suck up liquids

scavenger animal that feeds on waste or dead animals

shelter place that provides protection from danger or bad weather

Find out more

Books

Rat (Animal Neighbours), Stephen Savage (Wayland, 2007)

Rubbish Bins and Landfills (Horrible Habitats), Sharon Katz Cooper (Raintree, 2010)

Streets and Alleys (Horrible Habitats), Sharon Katz Cooper (Raintree, 2010)

Websites

See videos and read facts about rats at:
http://www.bbc.co.uk/nature/life/Brown_rat

Find out all about flies at:
http://www.pestworldforkids.org/flies.html

For ten fascinating facts about foxes go to:
http://www.allaboutanimals.org.uk/ PK-Favorite-Fox.asp

Index

above a bin 4-7
antennae 6, 15, 30
around a bin 22-23
at the top of a bin 10-15

babies 9, 25, 27
birds 5, 23, 26-27, 29

cats 23
chicks 27
claws 12
cockroaches 14-15, 26
cubs 25

deep inside a bin 16-21
dens 25, 30

eggs 9, 11

flies 8-9, 11
food 4, 5, 6, 7, 8, 9, 10, 11, 13, 14,
    15, 17, 19, 21, 23, 24, 26, 27
foxes 24-25

gnaw 13, 30
gulls 26-27, 29

habitats 4, 28-29, 30
hatch 9, 11, 30

insects 6-7, 11, 14-15, 30

maggots 11, 30
mucus 18, 30

nests 27

pigeons 5, 23
poo 15
prey 23, 30
proboscis 8, 30

raccoons 28
rats 12-13, 23
rubbish tips 29

scavengers 24, 26, 30
shelter 4, 10, 30
sludge 20
slugs 18-19
stings 7

teeth 13
tongues 7, 19

wasps 6-7
waste 5, 6, 8, 9, 11, 14, 15, 16, 17,
    19, 21, 22, 24, 26, 29
woodlice 17
worms 20-21